GW00359503

A MAN IS ONLY AS GOOD …

A POCKET SELECTED POEMS

'A MAN IS ONLY AS GOOD …'
is first published in 2017 by
Orange Crate Books,
Dublin, Ireland.

orangecratebooks@gmail.com

Copyright © Pat Boran, 2017

ISBN 978 0 9931726 1 8

⋇

Cover photograph
'Dog and Man on Burrow Beach'
by Pat Boran

⋇

ORANGE CRATE BOOKS
are available through
Dedalus Press, Ireland
www.dedaluspress.com

A MAN IS ONLY AS GOOD ...

A POCKET SELECTED POEMS

PAT BORAN

Orange Crate Books

ACKNOWLEDGEMENTS

This pocket-sized edition of the poems of Pat Boran significantly refines the selection from *New and Selected Poems* (Dedalus Press, 2007) and extends it with poems taken from his 2012 collection *The Next Life*. As such, with the exception of *Waveforms: Bull Island Haiku* (2015)—a book-length sequence which does not lend itself to excerption—the present volume draws on all of his publications to date, namely: *The Unwound Clock* (1990), the chapbook *History and Promise* (1990), *Familiar Things* (1993), *The Shape of Water* (1996), *As the Hand, the Glove* (2001) and *The Next Life* (2012).

Detailed acknowledgements and thanks are included in all of these earlier works, but the poet wishes to thank again the editors and publishers of the many publications and radio programmes where poems included here, or versions of them, originally appeared.

CONTENTS

✻

✳

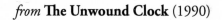
from **The Unwound Clock** (1990)

HOUSE

Water clanks from the tap
like a chain—a lifetime

since anything has moved here
but rats and birds. I see

the last inhabitants as a father
and son, the father

sending the son off to the city
with a handshake and a pocket

of old pound notes.
He might as well be sending him

to bring home the time
without a watch to carry it.

WIDOW, SHOPPING IN PORTLAOISE

She parked her black Raleigh
outside Whelan's butchershop
and bought her brother his chop.

The basket creaked with meat.

She orbited the roundabout
in the Market Square
and stopped there for bread

where a brown dog tore a refuse bag.
The cream on buns
yellowed in the sun
and tinsel paper caught dead flies.

A fridge purred the pleasures of a 99.
To "How's all at home?" she replied
"Fine", as if it were a brand name.

And then she cycled home again the pothole road,
breathing like an old engine,
whistling as she came through the gate exhausted
to see her brother shout abuse at a hen.

THE CASTLECOMER JUKEBOX

We often travelled to Garryhinch for turf,
my mining-town father and I,
kissing the wet road

in his lip-red Volkswagen van.
The song on his lips was always
Play To Me Gypsy—"beside

your caravan". How has it happened
that this is his only song?
Outside Kilkenny in two rooms,

eight boys and their six sisters
rearranged the contents of a home, and grew,
approximately, into each other's clothes.

Did they all have just one tune—
something popular in their youth become
the soundtrack for their lives?

A haiku-worth of *Play To Me Gypsy*
recorded by him in that house
with the outside toilet.

December, they stood side to side
or in a perfect vaudeville arc,
smiling, snow and stars outside.

And their parents, uncommonly relaxed,
crunching home-baked cakes like popcorn, tossed
a thrupenny bit giddily, hand to hand,

whispered together like teenagers,
selecting the Christmas Dinner song
from their barefoot Castlecomer Jukebox.

CAMDEN STREET IN THE MORNING

Camden Street in the morning, and a man
lifts a piano above his head,
emerging for a day he knows will offer
only rain and criticism:
You eejit, Paddy.
Eight hours of this await him
with reporters asking:
Can she be really worth it?

Even so
what do they know of his nights?
that tower of pianos silent to the moon?

MASTER

Drummer with a country & western band,
he was master
of the standard dowel.

Like a martial artist his arm became
a rope of steel:
I am no style

and I am all styles. Breath.
Then that polished blur
across my fingers,

snare, high-hat, snare, high-hat,
tom-tom, timbal,
side, bass, kettle drum
                    & cymbal.

THE LIVING ROOM

A one-time philatelist I kept the glass,
never one to allow anything which brought
the minute into view to pass.

Enthusiastic and in my prime,
I'd magnify the tiniest mass
ten, a hundred, a thousand times.

Huge were the rings of wood, the whirl
of fingertips, the amoeba's mime.
Still, the lure of something minuscule.

When the glass failed, my mind and will
persisted towards the molecule,
the atom magnified to fill

a cathedral, angels singing around
electrons, protons, the invisible
neutrinos. Even still, these sounds:

a candle sputtering in the gloom,
a fly declining solid ground,
you chuckling in the living room.

CITIES

We build our cities close to mountains,
for this: so that in brilliant sunshine
we may crawl and claw to the summits
to look out over the magnificent
transience of what we are.

CONCERT OFF KENSINGTON
HIGH STREET

By ten o'clock the site was alive:
Casey, the foreman, already chewing on his pencil,
a kettle boiled for the first strong teas,
and Cookey on the mixer had prepared
a wonderful cement that made the men's mouths
    water.

And high up in the scaffolding
Big Bill sang the blues,
balanced delicately on an old black bucket
that doubled as a piano stool.

By noon he had finished the wall,
tinkling the ivory bricks into place
with so passionate a history of Basin Street
that Casey made a collection among the crowd
in a riddle, directing latecomers from the street
with his No Parking megaphone
to the less desirable, cement-bag seats.

WHEN YOU ARE MOVING
INTO A NEW HOUSE

When you are moving into a new house
be slow to write the address in your address books,
because the ghosts who are named there
are constantly seeking new homes,
like fresher students in rain-steamed phone booths.

So by the time you arrive with your books
and frying pan, these ghosts are already
familiar with that easy chair, have found
slow, slow creaks in the floorboards,
are camped on the dream shores of that virgin bed.

HAVE YOU LEFT MOUNTMELLICK
FOR EVER?

Old yellow hut at the end of the garden,
jet sprays aerosol foam on the sky:
Have you left Mountmellick for ever?

The convent has me drunk on wine
uniforms, Maguire's dog snaps a trap
of teeth through their gaudy fence.

Have you left Mountmellick for ever?
The Christmas tree is still up—in April—
just a naked spear. I expect to see

the shrunken head of Christmas
or you continually zebra-crossing to make
the boys in leather jackets grit their teeth,

stamp their cigarette butts out and cry,
gulping back years of lust and tears:
Have you left Mountmellick for ever?

THE IMMORTAL

I'm Martin Drennan from Ballydavis,
tipping back glasses of Guinness
and whiskey in Dinny Joe's,

remembering the balls in the town hall
where I'd slip in unnoticed
to watch and drool

Woodbine ash from the balcony.
And out in the Market Square,
fresh with the smell of pigs,

before the Wright brothers
changed the dreams of men—
long before spluttering aeroplanes—

those arms of empty haycarts
looked like anti--aircraft guns,
aligned, jutting into sky,

and the spit-and-polish farmers,
always gaunt in monochrome,
scrutinised the camera

that captured for posterity
their endangered species—
the Irish between wars.

from **History and Promise** (1990)

SMALL TOWN LIFE

My neighbours escort
a body down the street,
a woman enclosed
with clothes—the first
and last gift of society. Wreaths
hint towards a relationship
between death and beauty,
as the mannequins,
their eyes open, dream
in the windows of a department store,
wearing the clothes we say we would die for,
and in which, any day now,
we may be buried.

THE FLOOD

Mrs. O has made a grotto
of her window ledge, saving first
the statue of the Virgin, followed by
a print of uncle John in '63,
a birthday card in crayon
from her nephew, her lilac blouse
and a jewellery box already rusting.

The boats that pass before her
have been disentangled from
the overgrown back gardens
of this nightmare Venice, this mockery
of the honeymoon she never had.
Oh that there had been time for uncle John …
Oh that Seamus Brennan had come back for her
    as promised …

Where are they now as the waters level off
and the boys in waders help to drag
the furniture outside? Now that the house is
    empty,
save for the smell of damp that will never leave.
Now that she must find another place to go—
having already packed for what she thought
would be her next and final departure.

A priest with a bucket slops about next door.
A local journalist photographs a fish.
Someone calls her name, but she ignores it.
History has returned to her midland town,
three hundred years after Cromwell's men,
and she is alone to face the interrogations.

LOWER MAIN STREET

i.m. Eddie Boylan

I remember your room and the table,
and your brother hovering about in the background,
the knots of knuckles in your fingers,
the way you eyed my cassette machine with
    suspicion.

But I do not remember exactly how I came to be
close to you in your final years, to coax you
back to when you were my age, a boy
in a turn-of-the-century midland town

where newspapers were the post-communion liturgy
at the back of church. And in the richness
of tea and grain—scents I did not recognise
then, nor have I since—we faced each other,

young men across a century of change, our town
outside your grocery shop transformed at such a pace
that, stepping out from your fading world, rich
in an obsolete currency, the notes

for that article in my hand—only
the butcher's greeting made me real in time
as the clocks of his hanged carcases dripped
seconds on the slab behind the glass.

A LOVER'S GRAFFITO

And what if all that survives of here—

    this squinting, twisted town of ours
    with its fortress prison and barricades,
    its three-storey street with two abandoned
    to storage space,
    the littered square,
    the motorway,
    Gandon's ruin,
    the new estates—

is this shed with the door kicked in,
a cider bottled, our scribbled names?

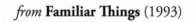

from **Familiar Things** (1993)

NIGHT

for Larry Cosgrave

Night, fog, ice on the road,
the town spirited away in this cloud
to where, just hours from now,
at dawn, with only our imperfect memories,
we must begin again, rename
the birds, the streets, the songs—in short,
all that we have known and would return us,
love permitting, to an image
of this earth for ever.

WAVING

As a child I waved to people I didn't know.
I waved from passing cars, school buses,
second floor windows, or from the street
to secretaries trapped in offices above.
When policemen motioned my father on
past the scene of the crime or an army checkpoint,
I waved back from the back seat. I loved to wave.
I saw the world disappear into a funnel
of perspective, like the reflection in a bath
sucked into a single point when the water drains.
I waved at things that vanished into points.
I waved to say, "I see you: can you see me?"

I loved 'the notion of an ocean' that could wave,
of a sea that rose up to see the onlooker
standing on the beach. And, though the sea
came towards the beach, it was a different sea
when it arrived; the onlooker too had changed.
They disappeared, both of them, into points in time.
So that was why they waved to one another.
On the beach I waved until my arms hurt.

My mother waved her hair sometimes. This,
I know, seems to be something else.
But when she came up the street, bright and
     radiant,

her white hair like a jewel-cap on her head,
it was a signal I could not fail to answer.
I waved and she approached me, smiling shyly.
Sometimes someone walking beside her might
wave back, wondering where they knew me from.

Hands itched in pockets, muscles twitched
when I waved. "There's someone who sees me!"
But in general people took no risk with strangers,
and when they saw who I was—or wasn't—
seemed relieved, saved from terrible disgrace.

Now it turns out that light itself is a wave
(as well as a point, or points), so though for me
the waving is done, it's really just beginning.
Whole humans—arms, legs, backs and bellies—
are waving away, flickering on and off,
in and out of time and space;
pushing through the streets with their heads down,
smiling up at office windows,
lying in gutters with their kneecaps broken
and their hopes dashed; driving, loving,
hiding, growing old, but always waving,
waving as if to say: "Can you see me?
I can see you. Still … still … still …"

BORN TO SHAVE

I'm so tall now at 28
the only thing I see is my chin,
the place where my head becomes lost
in my clothes and might be anybody's.
I look for myself in this mirror
and find only a chin, sometimes
a tooth, occasionally my tongue.

And so I wet my invisible face,
like someone blind apply, blindly,
the foam—resisting the chemical smell
until it dissipates—and bend my knees
an inch or three so that I know
it is me that I am shaving.
Born to shave.
           A child
looking in the same mirrors, I saw then
only ceiling, followed, years later,
by hints of hair, then eyes,
and then this chin. Born
to age and shave.
Born to grow up to face myself.
Born to regret and, in the light
of regret, to make promises, like this:

Years from now I'll reach
from some otherworldly place,
where none of this means anything, to touch
this hand-basin, these dulled blades.

4th September, 1991

CHILDREN

Children in ill-fitting uniforms
drive adults to school, and children
argue the cost of tobacco
in the Newsagent's nearby.

You must have noticed them.

And in the mornings they rise to slaughter pigs,
cook breakfast, solve crosswords at the office ...
Or they send tiny adults into minefields,
barefoot, with pictures
of Khomeini around their necks,
their old toes searching the sand
for death.

And children queue for Bingo
on Ormond Quay, on Mary Street,
and douse their leaking take-aways with vinegar.

And children talk and smoke incessantly
in Eastern Health Board waiting rooms,
always moving one seat to the right,
someone's parents squabbling over trinkets
on the worn linoleum.

And it is always children
who will swear for their tobacco—children
with beards and varicose veins—
and children, dressed as policemen,
who pull their first corpses from the river.

And who is it who makes love in the dark
or in the light, who haunts
and who does all our dying for us,
if not children?

We leave their fingerprints
on everything we touch.

ALWAYS BOOKS IN YOUR ROOM, MARGARET

Yet the books will be there on the shelves, well born,
Derived from people, but also from radiance, heights.
—*Czeslaw Milosz*

Always books in your room, Margaret:
I met Chaucer at your bedroom door
years ago. While dodging school
we faced each other an hour or more—
his language a foreign place.

Always books in your room, Margaret:
Yeats and Kavanagh stayed behind
awhile when you went off to college,
bearing—they never seemed to mind—
the lack of direction in my face.

Always books in your room, Margaret:
the feeling I had on Sunday drives
when you were home was that we shared,
though silently, in countless lives
across the world and down the years.

Always books in your room, Margaret,
and, little by little, books in mine.

Like the suburbs lurking in Coughlan's sandpit
when we were small, which, in their time,
found language for their hopes and fears,

the suburbs growing in my head,
populated by the real, the dead,
the imaginary, understand they owe
a debt to you. And their wish, so:
always books in your room, Margaret.

SONG FOR MY PARENTS

They're at home now, looking out at the evening,
hearing the floorboards creak, the distant
hum of factories. The town, the house
they hoped to pass to me, has changed.
The small routines of favour
to one butcher rather than the next
are fading. They forget
what they were about to say, and why.

Evening sky and age, you do not take them,
but rearrange the furniture of home
until they lose themselves among familiar things.

ANGELS IN LOVE

When angels fall in love
they dance on the heads of pins,
throw themselves into fireballs, or stay
underwater in the pool for hours.

Sometimes they even slash at their wrists
with razor blades or wood planes,
failing, of course, to tear the delicate skin.

For, in the absence of pangs, or flutters,
how else would they emulate our love?

BEDTIME AT THE SCIENTIST'S HOUSE

for Peter

Tell us again how the universe contains
no straight lines, though Saturn's rings
stay coin-thin to 500,000 miles.
Tell us that one again.
We always enjoy it.

Tell us the names of Jupiter's moons,
the valencies of atoms 1 to 103.
Illustrate constant random motion,
quasars on the brink of invisibility.

And show us, oh please, that picture
of a space-time world like a medicine ball
dropped in a net. Just once more,
softly, like music,
then we will sleep.

SEVEN UNPOPULAR THINGS TO SAY
ABOUT BLOOD

1.
Our mothers bled, and bleed,
and our enemies,
and our enemies' mothers.

2.
It rushes to the finest
nick, romances the blade.

3.
It dreams
the primary dream of liquids:
to sleep, horizontally.

4.
It is in the surgeon's heart,
the executioner's brain.

5.
Vampires and journalists
are excited by it; poets
faint on sight.

6.
I knew it better as a child,
kept scabs, like ladybirds, in jars.

7.
Blood: now mine would be with yours
until the moon breaks orbit
and the nights run cold.

THE MUSEUM OF THE NEAR FUTURE

In the museum of the near future
we walk around the exhibit of ourselves,
lips pursed, bent on stiff legs
to view the exposed undersides.
"Well, you seem to have gained a little weight,
though, yes, it probably is the light.
But what can I be thinking of—
those awful sideburns!" Never mind,
ours is a dance of cursory inspection.
Once we notice there's a party in the next room,
the thrill of being our own guests, of sticking
fingers in our own future wounds, wears off.
In moments we're like tourists without plans,
or manners, drinking all we can hold, stubbing
     cigarettes
into the carpet because, look, we won't be back!
And hey, if that security guard is leaving,
we could make love right here, right now,
next week's edition of *The Irish Times* beneath us …

Thrown out for causing a disturbance,
we stand in the rain, incredulous, soaked and
     sober,
shoelaces undone, our flies open,
the museum behind us impossibly grey.
"Are you ok?" You just can't help laughing:

"What was all that about?" you ask. We kiss.
It's hard to say, looking at your perfect face
and the already fading scars I glimpsed.

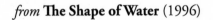

from **The Shape of Water** (1996)

ENTRANCE

It's like what happens with water,
a lake, for example,
which you open
slowly with your hands,

when you sigh, unintentionally,
at a concert recital,
and the breath seems
inseparable from the pain:

you're made human again.

FOR MY GOLDFISH, VALENTINE

Such enormous sadness
in such a tiny world.
And, looking down at you
in the water clouded
by your flaking scales,
I wonder if my impulse
to take you home
last Valentine's Day
(following a goldfish dream)
was not just the desire
to share my tenancy
of these dusk-facing rooms
under winter's hold.

That dream of gold.

You can imagine how it took me
back into my own smaller body
and bigger, child's imagination
when I found you too incarnate
in an earlier form.
As the lama recognises
his master in a child,
entering the pet shop
I knew you then at once—
the golden fish who swam

in the lens of my parents' house,
in the lens of my childhood,
before floating up one day
to leave that world as I
too left that world, as you
soon again must leave.
Today in the meantime
you look out at me
with the same bewildered eyes,
mouthing the same mute syllable,
the eternal Om that says
nothing changes.

Lead becomes gold and gold lead.
A child will be god when god is dead.

Soon I will recognize your replacement.

THEY SAY

The gun dog stole his master's gun
and tried to bury it in the garden,
which might explain the noise.

For something woke the entire household
eventually bringing the master himself
from his book-lined study in his nightshirt

and hob-nailed boots—somnambulist
of the quiet hours—clutching air
then stepping out, cautiously,

cautiously, beyond

the porch-light of language.

MOON STREET

1.
It's a minute to, a minute past,
but always the night of the sky,
the waxing or waning or full moon
here on Moon Street,

where every key fits every lock,
every heart is open or broken,
and posters of missing household pets
turn the railway station into a gallery

of loss. What's there to lose?
Come on, there's a party tonight.
Music waits to be released.
The windows are large enough to view

whole sweeps of sky, whole dusty
constellations too long swept aside.
Birds are singing when you arrive,
dancing, or exhausted, in Moon Street.

2.
In Moon Street when you meet she cries,
not on seeing you, but on not seeing
herself, as if a cloud had passed over
some taken-for-granted sphere, leaving

an inexplicable absence in the cosmos,
a strange wavering of otherwise perfect orbits.
But always you can feel that pull,
like the sensation of crossing someone's grave.

Moon Street. Could have called it
Ex-Girlfriend Street, but didn't.
Who could live there were there not
at least some small respite from ghostly visits?

3.
To give oneself completely
isn't wise. But wisdom isn't in it.
More footsteps have taken you to Moon Street
than dreams have shown you moons,

because you get there not by dreaming
but by walking in the wind or cold, or calm,
sometimes having washed, more often than not
ragged, worn and tired. You never realise

where you are going until you get there,
where nothing is planned, nothing is known,
and you're drawn back into the heart's old orbits,
tiny as a grain, massive as a moon.

WORDS

The answering machine
meets my arrival
with unblinking eye.
No word. Now even your voice
evades my traps.

*

Fintan the goldfish,
recently bereaved,
swims round in his world
of light, transparency,
searching for his shadow.

*

Turned sideways, the books,
face to face, square up,
insisting on their versions
of the same old story:
your life, my life.

*

The wine-coloured bedspread
contoured like an ocean;

the wind in the trees;
and your absence ... These nights
I flounder not swim.

*

The pièce de résistance?
Has to be this cup
with your lip-prints on it,
a tea-leafed shell
I hold to my ear.

*

Calling your name
in laneways only alcohol
knows the way back to.
Every cat knows you now.
Wild dogs remember me.

*

The hearth is always bare
in portraits of the Virgin
to signify virginity.
In mine a fire rages.
I'm burning your love letters.

*

My clothes on the floor,
my body in a twist,
my heart turning over and over
the same old question: whose
words are these anyhow?

*

The keyboard and mouse.
Or this old journal and pen.
At last, if only with fingers,
with fingertips, I'm feeling
for you again.

A CREATION MYTH

The story goes that Wheeler stepped outside,
as is the rule. Great physicist or not,
when you're having dinner at Lothar Nordheim's
you find that leptons, bosons, quarks and whatnot

tend to dominate. It's a relief
when someone suggests a party game. "The door,
Mr Wheeler. Twenty questions. I believe
everyone knows, as it were, the score."

Laughter. Wheeler's exit. A puff of smoke.
(I always imagine him smoking in the yard.
Great physicists or not, we're all plain folk
in sudden darkness where any light's a star

and stars mean company.) But what was he
    thinking of
as it dawned on him they hadn't called him back,
and time was fizzling out like the red dwarf
of his cigarette fading in the dark,

leaving him alone there with his god?
Or just alone … Time to go back inside.
Yet, as soon as he stepped in, the room seemed odd—
though it might have been the fact that he'd been
    miles

and years away, and now had to begin
all over, like some astronaut returned
to planet Earth and to these strange beings
who were, he knew—he told himself—his friends.

"Is it animal?" No. "Vegetable?" Well, he'd begun
at least, and, in the beginning anyway,
the others answered normally, but then one—
a colleague—faltered, couldn't seem to say,

for sure, yes or no, as if somehow
she didn't know herself! And that smoke again.
Now it doesn't take a physicist to know
when something's not quite right. Still, being trained

in logic means you don't like to concede,
so by the time he asked, "Is it a cloud?"
he already knew that's what it had to be,
and nothing else. And even as the crowd

composed themselves, and started to explain
their little joke—how they'd agreed not to consult
but just to play by ear—for Wheeler it was plain:
expectation determines the result.

LISTENING WIND

He crashed the car through the fence,
got out, calmly, picked up the fence,
turned it on its side, then climbed it,

a ladder into sky.
His parents were there before him,
Marie aged 7, Arthur 5.

Still calm, he took their hands.
A man in sandals and a dinner suit
led them through a door

into a wheat field. The words listening wind
came to him for a moment—words!—
then they were gone.

He was led to a garden swing
where he knew he was missing something—
his taunted, earth-bound shadow.

And then he awoke, with a start,
horn blowing, wheels spinning
in mud, wheels spinning in his heart.

CHAIRS

are used to make us sit, not to allow us
to be seated. In this sterile air
who would ever think to disobey
their unvoiced command, their four-square

authority? Just as dumbbells in gyms
test the strength of our devotion
to change, so chairs display our weaknesses:
our need for support, loss of orientation …

The music of the heart is piped through veins.
Until actors arrive the play can't run.
Snails, though always on the road, like poets
never leave home. And so cannot return.

These are our lived-for insights: but when it comes
nothing brings you down to earth like death,
and the wings of cancer angels tipped
with brown-sugared light like cigarettes …

And chairs are used to make us sit and think.
Still after still of the history of chairs
will show the unearthly stillness of their existence,
and ours by extension. So, prepare

for wards like these, long shining corridors,
and chairs, not in unassailable rows
but cooling and moving apart like separate planets,
fading into the luxury of shadow.

And though you feel one now against your arse,
nevertheless it is difficult to believe
chances are you will be in one, like my friend,
when you would slump, but for it, to your knees.

ENCOUNTER

Sometimes I like you, but I must confess
most of the time, old man, you wear me down,
slumped there in your chair like a sack
of my father's sacred potatoes back home

in a wintry light. And your so-called news,
that "It is, after all, what they said it would be."
What is? What all? And who said? Is this why
you asked me to come here, to sit and drink tea

and listen to riddles? And anyway who
do you think you are?—looking like the shade
of my own undead father. And when I offer you
a cigarette you don't even respond, instead

you draw yourself up so the light from behind
makes you appear paper-thin, like a leaf
from a Bible. Then, suddenly, finding strength,
just when I think it must be time to leave,

you're all advice: "Don't waste your middle years,"
you say. "Don't treat your life like one big joke."
But when you finally have to pause for breath,
I strike a match, and once again you're smoke.

AGE, LIKE A TRESPASSER

Age, like a trespasser, has crept
into your garden, has found
and sat down to your cigarettes,
exhaling the blue smoke of the future.
Look, now he is playing your guitar,
competent and in no hurry,
and now he is simply regarding the sky
as a man might regard his own hands.

Age, like a trespasser, has crept
into your garden, and the apples
fall directly from the trees,
one by one, into his open bag.
Listen, now against his idle whistling
you begin to hear your heart,
and now your dog is barking wildly,
troubled, frightened, by himself.

Age, like a trespasser, has crept
into your garden, and for the first time
you are not alone as the sun goes down
and familiar colours begin to fade.
Now is the time to confront the darkness
though you cannot see the apple blossoms.
Now you must remain quite calm
though from time to time he calls your name.

Age, like a trespasser, has crept
into your garden where it's night now and you sleep
like cat and mouse, wolf and sheep,
perfect and ancient foes.
But tomorrow, before first light,
stand there to gaze at him a while—
the crooked spine, those tired old limbs—
then tiptoe back into your woken life.

'IN HELL, ACCORDING TO GARY LARSON'

In hell, according to Gary Larson,
the maestro will spend eternity
in a room full of gap-toothed yokels,
straw in their hair, banjos on their knees:

And Bach, Shostakovich and Mahler,
and the first song he heard as a boy—
his mother singing Bizet in the kitchen,
shy both in her pain and in her joy—

and his father too the way he hummed those nights
when he had too much to drink, some tune
from his own dead father's lips, the very tune
he ceased to hum the day his fingers died,

the very tune which the night of his own funeral
came for the maestro like a fist of smoke
and dragged him up the chimney into darkness,
away from the attentions of the womenfolk,

beyond the streetlights, up beyond the city,
and down again into some distant room
waiting on the far side of memory
where his father was once again a groom

seated before the piano, and his hands
moved like the hands of a lover,
reaching out, feeling for another,
a New World—all will be forgotten.

For in hell, according to Gary Larson,
the maestro will spend eternity
in a small room full of sweaty yokels:
"Oh! Susanna, don't you cry for me …"

A REASON FOR WALKING

Words when I think,
thoughts when I word.
Hours with this thought only:
Only words,
not what I feel.

The streets offer
not promise, but escape.
Harmony Row, Misery Hill.
Any named place
better than this.

Back home, the summer sheets
an open book, if blank.
But then the light impression
of our bodies, curled up—
the hieroglyph for love.

UNTITLED

for Kaja Montgomery

Nothing is mine here
but the symbols of things—
doorways, streetscapes and wings
drawn on the footpath
by a traveller child who,
when the rain washes away his world,
sits up and sings.

HOW TO BE MY HEART

Become elastic,
enjoy the solo sound
as well as harmony.
Enjoy the fall—
don't expect ground.
Never move
but never quite be still.
See life as giving
rather than receiving
though the same blood passes
through your grasp like
rosaries, geometries, bound
infinities of love.

Be practical—work.
Keep the orchestra on course,
but imagine the clouds, the skies
you'll never see.
Learn trust. Don't mutiny
when I wade up to my chest in water.
Don't panic if I succumb to drugs
or drink. Don't sink.
Don't ache at every recollection
of a past populated by grief.
Don't succumb to disbelief.
Don't see only darkness up ahead.

Don't stay in bed all day.
Don't lie down and die.
Be there when I need the heart
to tell the unpalatable truth
or the necessary lie.
And give me the sensation of skydiving
when she so much as
walks into my sight.
Make haemoglobin
while the sun shines.
But keep a little oxygen aside.

ANSWERING MACHINE

A flashing light will mean I'm not alone.
A moment later maybe I'll hear your voice,
or that of a stranger, or the sound
of someone somewhere having second thoughts

and hanging up. But at least I'll know it means
that someone thinks about me, now and then,
and whoever they prove or do not prove to be,
at least there is a sort of consolation

in the fact that they send a gift of light,
a sign to welcome me on my return.
You are not alone, it will say, first thing,
the green light of the answering machine.

Or else: how desperate you've become
for love, the glimmer of surprise,
alone there in the doorway of your room
like a man before an endless, starless sky.

from **As the Hand, the Glove** (2001)

MILKMEN

The doorbell rings. I go.
I'm fourteen. That's how it is,
no need to stop or think.

It's the milkman's eldest son,
putting a brave face on it,
wearing his father's shade.

So quietly he pours the milk,
pours its at-first almost thin,
then rolled, then muddy sound

until the gallon is filled.
I close the door and wait
for the milk to settle down.

Years later—for it is years
already—I begin to know
what it means, this opening

of doors, of silences, to accept
things not made on the spot
but handed over: love, inheritance.

NO MAN'S LAND

The world began with our house.
At night if you listened hard
you could hear a whole universe
still forming. Out in the back yard

where the Milky Way stretched between
the roofs of cut-stone sheds,
bats flittered in the beams
of our flashlights, their tiny heads

like turned-out pockets. Closer,
water dripped or gushed, the dog
sensed something, cocked an ear
then stood as if the hands of a clock

had frozen somewhere. I was back
in No Man's Land again, a place
I loved, and feared: the black,
damp air pressed against my face

like a hand. Behind me at the door
separating inside and out,
womb and world, a dozen or more
slugs would gather, dumb, devout

as guard dogs, thick as eels
or old rope, drawn by the light

or warmth of the house, the wheels
and spirals of their journeys bright

as silver dust in honey. So when
the time came to go back, to leave
that strange land, head down I ran
as fast as I could, leaping clear

of the lair of teeming serpents, and with luck
making it across the threshold
into human light again, awe-struck
by strangeness, bringing strangeness home.

HALL OF MIRRORS

"I'd like …" says the stranger standing before me,
  "that!"
He points to something over my shoulder and waits.
It's a Travel Agency, though my father calls it
  The Shop,
and brochures that glisten with pictures of girls in
  all states

of undress, stretched on white sands or by pools,
cover the walls and counters behind me. I know
without looking round. But when I reluctantly do
(awkward teenage), it's something I've not seen
  before:

he's pointing to a small gold mirror containing
a fish-eye microcosm of the room we're in.
It's like the room in Van Eyck's Arnolfini Wedding
except, of course, I'm in V-neck and flares, and, thin

as a rake though I am, sport a Bruce Lee medallion.
It's important to face the world with an iron will.
So, to this strangely familiar stranger's reflection
I say, "Sorry, but that mirror is not for sale."

But before I can explain this is a Travel Agency,
a place you go when you want to go some place,
and not some newsagent's or hall of mirrors,
my father comes out and says, "Good man, you're
      there."

And in an instant it's just the two of us alone.
The stranger has vanished, as in Abracadabra.
It's the 1970s still, and all I know
begins with Abbey Road and ends with Abba.

DOORS AND WINDOWS

My father sold them, doors and windows,
entrances, exits, idyllic views
from houses not constructed yet
though mapped out with such absolute

precision that those wooden frames
we'd spend evenings stacking to the sky,
then half days driving and unloading
in windswept fields, before our eyes

transformed. Fingers smarting
from the rasp of wood, I'd press
a fist into a palm, count to ten
and watch my breath trace silent protest

in the air, then count to ten again
while he, as I now know, in his own way—
saliva in his palm—secured the deal
and made a friend he hoped would some day pay,

though many never did … Then we were off,
the builders stood there, watching through the glass
that wasn't even in those windows yet, and overhead
the Milky Way already settling into place.

NEIGHBOURS

They were the ones we told jokes about,
the red-necked, spud-thick family up the road:
how she smashed the car into the gate
going for her driving test, how once the door
came away in the father's hand like a sheet

of old wallpaper. And then their kid.
Helping daddy one day paint the fence
around their concrete garden, he knocked the tin
then ran away in tears, his yellow footprints
and their yellow footprints all over the street

like a dance-step map. Wee Johnny,
which is what they called him, never seemed
quite right after that. The poor wee mon, he
was frightened of his shadow. At Hallowe'en,
kids knocked on their door and threw him money

to see if he'd cry. Which he always did.
In school they ganged up on him in the yard
and made him sing The Sash. More than once he peed
his pants. More than once his furious dad
had to come and take him home at speed.

When the sister married, true to form
the old man drank so much he fell face first

into the wedding cake. The honeymoon,
in Ballyshannon, was a total farce:
the groom met an old flame and he was gone.

Their flat-faced dog liked to chase parked cars.
The mother opened doors in her dressing gown.
We laughed till we were sick, and then we laughed
even more. The day before they finally left town
the kid came second in a boxing match.

FLESH

The spirit, despite bad press,
loves the flesh.

It enjoys nothing more
than body odour,

the warmth of a crotch
or the electric touch

of lips. Those dark religions
which have banned the nether regions

to the netherworld, to hell,
can cast all the spells

they like, can single out for blame
those who refuse to feel shame

about their bodies—children, the old,
the 'savage' inhabitants of the Third World,

but most of all those women of loose morals
whose torture is somehow part of the quarrel

about sanctity and sin
and the vessels the soul is to be found in.

Enough idols and bones!
Enough gleaming chalices and altar stones!

I say it again: the spirit loves
the flesh, as the hand the glove.

And if you doubt me, ask my dying father
which he would rather:

to be done at last with love and pain,
or to leave, but then come back to flesh again.

AM

i.m. Nicholas Boran

1.35 a.m.
I look at my watch and see
my life story:
I thirty-five am.

And if I press this button here
I get the date, 1999,
the year when my *am* begins to mean
something new, something else,
your *was*, your *is no longer*,
the year of your death.

FOR S WITH AIDS

1.
When a star dies, my love, my man,
when it gets so tired, burnt out, so heavy,
it starts to fall back into itself,
it starts to grow in density, shrink
until, at last, there comes a time
when light escapes from it no more,
when time means nothing any more,
when science, naming and love itself
wring their hands at the hospital door.
Nothingness, absence, passing, loss …
our secret, sleeping partners, S.

2.
Ouroboros, mythological serpent
consuming itself, renewing itself,
the snake of Eden, snake of the tree,
the serpent coiled round the staff of being
still found on local chemists' signs,
like the one where you binged on vitamins—
what was it, three years back?—all set
to fight what you were sure was 'flu,
then toothache, backache, headache, gout …
Now your name cannot be spoken here
in these half-lit corridors leading nowhere
but I can hear your playful hiss,
snake brother, snake lover, S.

3.

Close up, the red-shift of apple skin
is a microcosm of the universe,
at once unbounded and finite.
See, what they did not tell us, S,
was that in Eden there were many trees
and many apples on their boughs,
on the skin of each whole galaxies,
in the core a constellation of seeds.
Unpicked the apple would still have fallen
to return to death and be born again
in whole new trees, in each apple of which
new seeds, new orchards, whole new Edens.

PS—And S, the snake's sloughed skin
is what he was, or will be, not what he is.

UNBUILD

I think the stairs bare.
I recall the tacks,
all three boxes we whacked
into them back there,

back then in the past, now
all for one and one for all
drawn out, withdrawn, or—
the right word—recalled.

Then the stairs itself.
From the corridor of space
I remove the zigzag shelf
down which I raced,

up which I crawled
when packed off to bed.
And now when night falls
I go back again

to unbuild the house.
Stone by blessed stone
I have taken it apart,
and still it is not gone.

LITERATURE

His penis hanging between his legs
like a vandalised telephone, or some
deep-sea creature that cannot bear
solitude, so it hangs on,

this naked man is what I am—
and yet how unlike me he seems,
surprised in this mirror I was dashing past
on my way through the house at 4 a.m.

And when a light comes on somewhere,
quick as a flash he turns away
like a man who would keep his truth concealed,
this Rosebud, this Jekyll, this Dorian Gray.

MACHINES

One night in York Street
almost ten years back—so much
drink and junk around the place

it was hard to say
just who was us, or them—one night
as I lay down to sleep on my own

cold slab of light, it started up:
below in the street, a car alarm
wielding its terrible, surgical blade

of sound. Across the way,
the College of Surgeons grinned in the night
like a skull, like a stack of skulls,

but it was hard not to cheer
when someone from a few doors up
suddenly appeared. A yard brush

like a weapon in his hands, he climbed
onto the gleaming bonnet where he stood
and began to swing,

first with aim and intent, so that
one by one the front lights went in, then
the indicators, the windscreen wipers,
      the windscreen itself …

and then, like some half-man, half-thing,
swung, swung, swung, swung,
swung till his muscles must have ached,

till the mangled brush tumbled from his grip
and he stopped, turned, looked up at us and roared
as if his spirit could no longer be contained

by the silence, by the darkness,

by the slow-motion tragedy of
so much of Dublin back in those
and still in these dehumanising days.

THE WASHING OF FEET

It's the simplest form of healing:
late at night,
the washing of feet.

When the light called sky
is an absence,
when the traffic's asleep;

when song
is a physical thing
needing physical shape

but you're just so worn out
facing darkness again
and those brave

tulips and roses
in Merrion Square
have long since turned in

to the dark, cottony
breath that simmers
inside of them.

When the world
is a cave, is a dungeon,
when the angels retreat,

return to this tiny
pacific ocean,
to the washing of feet.

TEARS

I like to cry,
I like to cry so much
first thing I did when I was born
was cry,
cry up a storm,
cry up
two small torrents,
two strong currents.
The world
slapped me as a signal
to begin
so I began
as I determined to continue
with tears.

All through my childhood years
I cried, sometimes
howling my release,
my relief,
my glad return
to this vale of tears.
Right up until
the time
the hormones came
out of hiding
out of waiting

and began
their slow tour of my body
tears
came easily.

Then in my teens
they stopped. My tears
went underground,
like the small stream
I'd played in as a boy
before our town grew up.
I knew they were there.
I felt their pull,
their attraction, but found
neither spring nor river mouth
where they might whisper
back to the greater
rhythm of ocean,
the ocean of tears.

No tears for instance
at seventeen
where there was more
to cry about
than I could explain,
and far too few
in recent years
when the brightest light

in the night sky
began to fade.

But now
I'm always close to tears,
at home with tears,
and not just mine but yours as well,
my love. I see or hear
or somehow sense
that hot swell as I cross a room
and pass a stranger in the street
as if all eyes
were forcing me to recognise
that something in the air.

And I have seen myself
in the future, prepared
to move on, move out
of the way, of the room,
through doors maybe
but back to a place
where tears are rolling
down my face
as the world lifts
its hands from my flesh
and I am lighter, I am light again,
and the sound of that

original slap
runs backwards before
all is still again,
all is quiet again
and my eyes sit still
in my skull again,
only salt now, dry salt now,
where once there were,
I'm glad to say,
my tears.

STILL LIFE WITH CARROTS

When I discover a carrot, like this one,
grown old, forgotten on a shelf
behind bottles of oil, herbs and spices,
all those nouveaux arrivés, I feel myself

drawn to it. It's as if all
the wonderful meals my life has been made of,
the exotic tables at which I have sat
had never existed, as if during love-

making a former lover had come
into my mind, or a neighbour, long dead
had knocked on the door and let himself in,
as of old, trailing the earth from his grave.

The politeness accosts me. Almost as frail
as my father in his hospital bed
those last long months, this carrot seems
to have something to tell me. The fact is, in the end,

the formidable weakens, the once proud
become stooped and sad. The lost
no longer recognize themselves.
And so it goes for all our vegetable loves:

the pea dries up; the tomato weeps
and weeps an ectoplasmic mess;
lettuce browns like an old book;
potatoes send up flares of distress;

but carrots just age there, waiting to be found,
as the plates on the table, like the planets, go
    around.

A NATURAL HISTORY OF ARMED CONFLICT

The wood of the yew
made the bow. And the arrow.
And the grave-side shade.

PENKNIFE

Still smelling of oranges
after years in this drawer
among buttons, paperclips,
envelopes, old specs …

a present from you;
designed to sever,
it's the one thing
that somehow connects.

LOST AND FOUND

Sometimes now I see my father
up in Heaven, wandering around
that strange place where he gathers up
what other souls no longer want,
as all his life he gathered
unloved things.

As if on a screen I see
his big frame bend, his bony hands
reach down for a rusted pin,
a nail, a coin from some lost kingdom.
One day it will be the very thing
someone will need.

And when the tears become too much
and this damned bed might be a field,
I sit up wondering how the hell
the world can always find more fools
to lose things and be lost themselves
and carry on.

Then something in my heart gives in,
and I know, as if I'd always known
deep down, that all that trash, that old
Christmas wrapping, those balls of string,
the belts, belt buckles, the left-hand gloves,

the dozens of pairs of worn-out shoes
and toeless socks, the blown light bulbs,
the coils of wire and threadbare screws,
the broken clocks, the plastic bags
folded neatly, the leaking pens
and dried-up markers, the ink-stained rags
and blotting paper, the bashed-in tins
of washers, plasters, needles and lint
were never his at all, were meant
for me.

FETCH

Again and again she comes back to me
to place it by my feet, today's
old piece of flotsam or bonfire debris
dug out from the heap and blessed
with a kind of magic.

Dog-given, the least of things
can be treasure for a day.

And how she spends these days,
this love-struck mutt,
stretched out along a neighbour's wall,
comically shadowing the postman,
or, despite the wind and ice-flecked rain
that keeps every other dog indoors,
bounding out across this desolate park
as if it were a summer's meadow, alive
to the possibility of play.

Hours, I imagine, she has spent already
running like this between her home
and mine, her world and ours,

to bring me a stick,
to chase that stick, to seize that stick

and then come back with that stick so tight
between her jaws it sometimes seems
she will never release it, that she has changed
the rules and very purpose of the game,

and had I the strength
I might lift her clear
or she might lift me clear
of this rain-locked planet.

TENT

Maurice has lost his virginity
in a tent, or so he claims, out beyond
the new hotel with a foreign girl
who happened to be hitching through.

When the jeering has at last died down,
most of us grin, kick at the earth
or stare into the middle distance, shy
of being the first to give himself away.

That evening, like tourists on a trail
to some historic battleground, we troop
all the way out, the full mile or more
to the now famous field where the girl is

long since gone, though yes there does appear
to be a faint impression in the grass:
rectangular, for all the world like a door
and big enough for a man to pass through.

THE ENGINE

With a four-sided aluminium key
and one hand clamped around the wheels
to hold them still, I hold my breath
and wind the engine of the small grey train.

I am five or six years old and I wind
for the soft creaking of the spring,
for the pull of these four small wheels
like the heart-throb of some living thing.

Later when I carve my name in wood
or later again stub out cigarettes
it will be with this same motion, but for now
I wind to be here, beside myself,

and with the last possible, last permissible turn
to release the perfect single ping
then watch as the engine heads out with the news,
a thing beyond me, a thing singing.

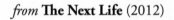

from **The Next Life** (2012)

WORM SONG

Articulated
servant of the plain truth
seldom stated,

part link, part chain,
serpent echo
in the slow lane

though sawn in half
on your journey
to the heart

of darkest matter. O lonely
shunting of the earth song
too low to sing; O hole

in the ring; O dull
but faithful sexton
of hallowed ground,

of growth and change,
pushing ahead
(again, and still again)

to where the sun
can never enter
though the rain seeps in—

O mindless worker,
blind muck-raker,
self-buried miner,

in your endless night
unmake all this, we pray,
to make it all alright.

SNOWMAN

No matter that we prayed
to God himself (father, son
and holy ghost), as well as half a dozen saints
we knew by name and some
odd talent or disfigurement—
the power to raise the dead,
to put out fires with their breath
or balance all night up a pole—
the meltdown came.

The head was first to go,
the belly lost a pound or two,
an eye came loose, the carrot nose
slipped an inch then disappeared
entirely overnight: perhaps a rat
or early bird had dragged it off.

Before we knew it
snowman became snow-thing,
stooped and hunched, a drunk
in a dirty linen suit, a gatecrasher
who'd lost his way, forced to spend the night
outside alone. Who could love him any more?
Even the crozier that made him seem
so wise last week—our own St. Patrick—
lay now like a question mark at his feet.

THE ISLAND

for Bob Quinn

Remote, solitary, its back to its neighbours,
facing instead the broad Atlantic and the dream
of a bright New World, that unkempt heap
of sand set down in our back yard by a builder

in the early 1970s became, the afternoon
he failed to show, our own small island: bays
and mountains, the major rivers, greys
instead of forty shades of green. Immune

to damp and cold, down on our knees
like the migrant workers of a generation before,
we laboured beyond nightfall until a door
in the darkness opened and saw us lifted clear

of our obsession. But who could sleep that night
leaving our small-but-perfect local wonder
with no one to defend it, alone there under
a cloud-marbled sky? Moonlight

flooding the house, I crept back down to check,
and found, to my astonishment, a fleet of snails,
like so many Norse or Spanish or Phoenician sails,
their glistening trails criss-crossing the hostile dark.

SPACE TRAVEL

In my school friend's back yard,
among the crates and silver kegs of beer
I never saw the promised corpse.

But on one occasion I recall,
fascinated by their gleaming hearse
under a soft fall of rain, we snuck

into the family workshop. *Keegan & Sons,*
the signboard proclaimed, *Publicans
& Undertakers.* We were ten,

but out there in that dim-lit space,
made brave by laughter we clambered in
and stood, in silence, side by side,

in two open coffins, rough-planed and propped
against a wall. Whole minutes passed,
neither of us wanting to be the one to break

the spell. Now thirty years have gone,
and I'm home to take my first ever drink
in the family pub, at his father's wake.

*

Biers & spirits; stiff ones and stiffs ...
The old jokes come back to haunt
at every return or passing visit.

The old doubts, too. Is that how it was?
Did we go, or only dream we could?
Yet another adventure never begun ...

Last night on my way up town
I stopped to stare into that off-street darkness,
and wondered how we would have looked

back then, back there, had either one
of our now late fathers happened past—
two small-town youngsters with time on their
     hands,

stood on the launch pad like astronauts,
ready for the journey to a better world,
schoolbags heavy with oxygen on our backs.

THE REED BED

The reeds that grew along the banks
of my first real love, the local stream,
generations back were prized

for basket weaving, mats and thatch
durable and waterproof
as any roof of slate or tile

a man might raise above his head.
Reed paper, it is said,
sufficed when better stuff proved scarce,

and the nibs of pens, themselves from reeds,
made reed-upon-reed the perfect match—
nothing between the two but air.

These last few nights, reeds everywhere
when I close my eyes and start to drift,
home after years in the reed bed

of childhood, carried aloft
to where reeds are plaintive in the breeze,
trout and minnow have not yet lost

their struggle to survive, and men on the run,
hidden in shallows till the bloodhounds pass,
peaceful as infants breathe through hollow reeds.

FAITH

Pushed out of the boat, my father
like so many of his siblings learned to swim
out of necessity. He'd seen, no doubt,
a sack of cats go down into the same

Dinin River, and might well have dreamed
the blackness at the far end of that string
of beads, those seeds of air that rose
to bloom and blossom on the water's skin.

And perhaps that helped. More likely though,
fear moved faster through his veins
than any conscious thought, and he was
kicking water, grasping, gulping air

almost before he knew he'd been pushed in,
his father extending from that small craft
an arm or splintered oar with which
to fish him out, still gasping, into an ark.

'UP THE ROAD'

Up the road and around the bend,
beyond the oak tree and the old shed
where Fionn MacCumhaill once spent a night
or we holed up one evening in the yellow light

of a thunderstorm, at the edge of town
where trucks change gear, where sense breaks down
and the whole broke country was showing off its
    veins
to the needle of the Lord, that's the place

you'll dream about, you're reaching towards
when darkness flares, when you choke on words
in the middle of nowhere, the place you'll miss
when the next life begins and you look back on this.

MATCHBOX WHEELS

i.m. Billy Brophy

From Stradbally he came—half a day's ride
on our 'high nellies'—in a small case
two or three dozen matchbox trays
we'd never see again in the same light.
One tray slotting neatly into the next,
his careful step-by-step progression turned
in on itself until the last and the first
completed the circle, and he taped them down.
Those matchbox wheels, we played with them
    for days,
an idea whose time had at long last come
to our sleepy, landlocked, midland town,
our ancient creaking vessel of a home
where two wonders arrived that same afternoon,
the Renaissance and the Industrial Revolution.

THE PRINCESS OF SORROWS

i.m. Michael Hartnett

The Princess of Sorrows blames herself
and cannot disguise it. For too long now
she has sat on this footpath and no longer recalls
the way home. In the hostel she feels
she will one day be invisible, not least to herself.
On nights like this only a doorway
seems solid. So five nights a week
she comes to sit here, her head to one side,
as though the fall or the blow
that has scarred her nose since yesterday
had snapped her neck. Rag-doll princess,
inner child of the inner city
set adrift, I touch your sleeve,
I drop a note in your paper cup;
I greet you in English, in Irish, in Greek,
or something that sounds like Greek; I speak
Lorca's Spanish, the Latin of Catullus,
two or three words of Romanian learned
one night in a bar from two drunken thieves
equally lost … And then it ends, passes,
the dance that's inside me, and I tip
the tip of my cap, clicking my heels
like poetry's Fred Astaire, and bow
low before you in inherited shame

at having so little to offer you here
on this Baggot Street night, in this Baggot Street rain,
where the cars flow past in a river of lights,
and we are not strangers, not any more,
but the Princess of Sorrows and Hartnett the poet,
each of us homeless in every language known.

'DREAM OF THE SPARROW MORNING'

Dream of the Sparrow Morning:
a line from some imagined Chinese poem,

a fragment of wisdom,
blurred by translation,

or something glanced at, flicked past
in a bookshop somewhere
years ago,

and forgotten
until now,

comes back to you,
come back *for* you,

wakes just before you do
in the dawn light,
to whisper in your ear.

And the more you think on it,
puzzle over it,
the more the phrase
professes no great
interest in meaning.

Dream of the Sparrow Morning:
five words having found each other,
a burst of colour on a hillside field,
the wild flowers of language.

And yet, now, watch as they lend themselves,
title-like, to everything you see:

your shirt and jeans draped over the chair,
your shoes standing by to useless attention,
your curled-up wristwatch on the bedside table,
foetal, like you and, like you, blank in the early light.

Dream of the Sparrow: Morning.

Dream of the Sparrow-Morning.

Or, my favourite:
Dream of the Sparrow (comma) Morning,
an exhortation, a prayer of breath,
a call for this bright morning to produce
that brown-grey plump-breasted short-tailed bird
whom Sappho imagined
drawing Aphrodite's chariot
across the heavens.

So, Dream of the Sparrow, Morning,
the soft landing of that comma
somehow perfect,

(the happy accident of its worm-like appearance)
as you draw the curtains this morning to reveal
the lawn outside and find the sparrows
already settled in, all business,
dreamt up by morning, conjured by it,
and making the most of the light.

INTRUDER

He doesn't recognize me, this scrawny kid
a few summers back still mowing lawns
for pocket money, now suddenly reborn
as the local tearaway, his shaved head
exposed in the full-moon beam of my flashlight
to the rear of the house, the world fast asleep,
autumn yet, by a thread, by the skin of its teeth.

"Looking for my ball," he says, matter of fact,
defiant, in his hand, half on show,
a bat or something heavier proposing
the alternatives. "At this hour?" I laugh
and stand my ground, part fool, part sage,
wondering what else might lie within reach
in the inky dark that floods the moment's page.

He sniffs, shifts uneasily, never looks away.
It's as though he's faced me a dozen times before,
the drunken father staggering through the door
at closing time, fists raised, shouting obscenities
for the whole estate to hear. Silence. A grunt,
then he's over the six-foot wall in a judder
of branches and shadows, less like a creature

fleeing than a creature in flight, the night air
electric, the garden alert to the brim

of the fence posts, the cap-stones, the tendrils of
   clematis
inching up through the stars ...
                             In the flickering dark
I wait for the echo of footsteps retreating,
hear nothing at all. Instead, like a picture
taken from orbit, there's us here, this youngster
and my middle-aged self, two figures bent double,
catching our breaths, one stood in grass
neatly trimmed, the other in splinters of glass
from a dangling street-lamp, hearts pumping
faster than lovers', the wall here between us
ungiving (yes), alien (surely), and cold to the touch—
not living (of course) and yet somehow
bristling with gooseflesh.

SKIPPING

Intense as a character in a fairytale
a small girl skips in the street
outside our house. For most of the morning
she has been there, skipping and singing to herself,
now with a friend, now with a gang of friends,
now on her own. Each time the rope comes round
she lifts herself up out of her shadow
with just a flick of her toes, and whether friends
return to chant some muddled rhyme
no small girl ever really understands
or worries much about,
or whether the ice-cream van trawls by,
slows down, tinkling its promise,
on she goes, skipping and leaving the world
over and over, loving
the weight of herself, the weightlessness,
the swoosh of the rope.

CORNER BOYS

The toughest man in town is now a granddad,
and every morning, his teenage daughter back
at secondary school, the local dogs
set free to chase each other through the park,

a vision in tattoos and knee-length shorts—
half pirate, half fairground muscleman—
he's out to push a Dora the Explorer pram
the length of the terrace, stopping to complain

about his lot, the dogs, the litter everywhere,
to pick a broken bottle off the road
and chuck it in a bin, and, now and then,
to stand his ground and share a grim-faced joke

with another crew-cut granddad like himself,
thirty years ago his mortal foe,
the pair of them there like boxers squaring up,
comparing snapshots on their mobile phones.

LET'S DIE

"Let's die," I say to my kids,
Lee aged five, Luca not yet three,
and under an August blanket of sun
we stretch out in the grass on a hill
to listen to the sea just below
drawing close, pulling back,
or to the sheep all around us
crunching their way down towards earth.

"Do you love the clouds, Dada?"
"Do you love the Pink Panther?"
and "Will you stay with us for ever?"
to which I reply, without hesitation,
Yes, Yes and Yes again,
knowing that as long as we lie here
everything is possible, that any of the paths
up ahead might lead us anywhere
but still, just in time, back home.

Like me, sometimes they act too much,
filling the available space and time
with fuss and noise and argument,
but up here, overlooking the landscape,
the seascape, of their lives, on this hill
they like to play this game, to lie
together and together to die

which, in their children's language, means
less to expire or to cease
than to switch to Super Attention Mode,
to prepare for travel, to strap oneself
into the booster seat and wait and wait
for the gradual but inexorable lift
up and off and out into motion.

For my two boys, things are only
recently made flesh, made mortal—
our uprooted palm tree, two goldfish,
the bird a neighbour's cat brought down
last week—and they are almost holy
with this knowledge. "Let's die now,
then let's go home for tea," Lee says,
putting into words as best he can
the sea's helpless love affair with the land.

LEARNING TO DIVE

The boy who is learning to dive
has a lot on his mind:

how to place
his unfamiliar, disobeying feet
on the slippery rungs;

how to straighten himself and walk
the length of the board
without glancing down;

how to stand, to extend
his arms straight ahead, as the other boys do,
without wavering;

how to cancel the height,
the shake in his legs,
once more how to breathe.

But while he stands there and the water stills,
from out of nowhere a kid half his size
goes charging past

to pedal pedal pedal in empty air,
before dropping right through into the target
of his own reflection. Resounding cheers,

upon which the older boy gives up,
surrenders to something somewhere
beyond his control

and at last steps clear
to fall
away into the rapturous applause

of water, each glistening drop
a medal struck to honour
the triumph of his simply letting go.

THE APPLE TREE

We bought it in the supermarket,
that flap-ended flexing limb of wood,
believing ourselves its liberators,
like blacked-up intruders who release
laboratory rats, setting off for home,
the thing stretched over the back seat
a tree in name alone, a patient
in the ambulance the car had become,
the city we passed through a landscape now
of concrete and steel, towers of glass
blankly watching as we blazed past.

At home we unwrapped and washed it slowly,
put it in a tub the kids packed
with compost, twigs and sympathetic magic—
a plastic soldier, some candies, small stones—
stroking the few wan leaves. Inside a week
new shoots appeared, a lifeless knot
puckered, stuck its tongue out, broke
into white flower. We laughed at our luck:
the dream of fruit, and we so far from Eden.

And when that first apple at last appeared
from behind a leaf—the first and last
as it transpired, like an only child—
it was as though the sun had singled out

our small back yard, that one dull tub
and sickly tree for special favour,
a starring role in the experiment of life.

LAWNMOWER MAN

Midway along a trench of grass
the lawnmower dies. A breeze
nudges the grassheads;
the metal casing ticks and cools,
imitating life. Perched
on the garden slide, the kids look on
in silence, and I become
before their eyes
the grandfather I never knew,
his old mule fallen to its knees
in a field where God
has turned up the volume
of the smallest things:
birdsong, the shift of grass-
stalk against stalk, middle age's
first appearance in the play,
these puzzled standstill moments,
those whisperings off stage.

A DOG

for Paula and Theo

A dog is a judge.
You cannot lie to a dog.
Even when you do not speak
a dog can hear you.

Like the house you grew up in,
or the concrete shed
on the windy side of school,
dogs have no time
for who you think you are
or plan to become.
They exist in the world
of the moment.
Hours, days and years
mean nothing to a dog.

Like that overgrown plant
out the back, or the shirt
upstairs still in its Christmas wrapping
seven months on, a dog
is always waiting
for your return.

Then it's the soul of the universe,
its eyes are twin black holes
drawing in and pouring out
primordial stuff. Hearts
are broken and remade
with one look from a dog.

And there is nothing in its power
a dog would not do, if it could,
for the one who shows it kindness,
stick-chasing and dancing,
lifting the regal paw, melting
like slush over the kitchen floor
to sleep the one-eye-open
finding-the-right-position-still
sleep of the just.

Yet it is one of the great sorrows
with which we humans must contend
that dogs can report so little
though they see so much.

What we would know
of the world, of existence itself,
if only we could converse with them,
these friends who learned to bark
to assuage our loneliness,

these damp-smelling angels
who suffer our moods and our scoldings
and still, in the end—
the table cleared and lights turned off—
who lead us out one final time
to stand in the darkness
and wait, looking up
like shepherds beneath
the canopy of the stars.

THAT PAIN

that comes and goes in the lower right,
the lower left; that stabs and throbs
and burns and leaves then comes again
and, at night, again;

that tight almost white vibration
in the ear; that string of sound
that ties you up and down, that binds
and won't let go; that slow
withering irritation; the deep
plunge in the heart, the steep
and sudden fall-off from the shelf
of stand-up, stand-still,
face-front, eyes-to-the-sky
persistence;

that sense of something
missing, something broken,
something killed;

that nothing good or willed; that sudden
drop in the surge of the blood, that
gasping for breath or grasping for support;
that impulse for fight
or flight, that fright—

that's when you vow to live.

HAIKU

First day back at work,
muttering, dragging his feet—
the method actor.

DURING THE WAR

We met, fell in love, set up home,
while the world prepared for war.
As battleships took up positions off the coast,
we began to clear the spare room.

They cut power lines, we laid carpet.
They jammed radio signals, we whistled to ourselves,
lifting floorboards, stripping paint and paper,
and each night falling into bed exhausted,
content with these brief glimpses
of a better world to come.

On the day the first bombs fell on Baghdad,
we finished what would be the nursery,
imagining the progress of tiny feet
as the stretcher-bearers set off
into a world of dust.

And a few years later, on the very day
six schoolkids died in Sadr city,
torn apart by a bomb that left
a hole six foot deep in the road,

we went to the zoo on our first big outing,
stopping before the well-kept cages,
waving at the animals, pulling faces,
trying out the noises we took to be their words.

'A MAN IS ONLY AS GOOD'

A man is only as good
as what he says to a dog
when he has to get up out of bed
in the middle of a wintry night
because some damned dog has been barking;

and he goes and opens the door
in his vest and boxer shorts
and there on the pock-marked wasteground
called a playing field out front
he finds the mutt with one paw

raised in expectation
and an expression that says: Thank God
for a minute there I thought
there was no one awake but me
in this goddamned town.

REVENGE

Lear went mad, Heathcliff prowled the moors,
and the militants built home-made bombs in sheds
identical to ours: old rusted tools
hanging from the beams, an ancient bicycle
half buried under bags and bric-à-brac,
and, on a bench, covered with a hessian sack,
enough fire power to take a child's face off.
Blow winds and crack your cheeks ... We read that
again and again, as if somehow the words
through repetition alone would start to make sense.

BARGAIN HUNTER

Talk-box, squawk-box … The other day
I found an antique wireless
in a local jumble sale,

the lacquer scarred, the dial stiff
and grating, the entrails scarcely contained
by the duct tape plastered across the back.

But could it work? I turned a knob:
a valve glowed orange, a whooshing noise
conjured the void, then a male voice spoke

clear and authoritative, not the words
I'd half-expected ("… *consequently*
this country is at war … ") but instead

"Ireland returns to world markets,
Taoiseach rules out default on bonds,
Health service closures cripple nation."

I turned it off, and tried a helmet on.

IMMIGRANTS OPEN SHOPS

i.m. Sargon Boulus, Iraqi poet (1944 – 2007)

Immigrants open shops, Sargon says.
In countries where they take in refugees,
that's what they do, they open shops.
To sell something, there's no real need to speak;

someone enters, points at 'this and that'
or finds what he wants on a shelf,
and all you need is half a dozen words
to serve him, 'yes', 'no', 'seven', 'Euros', 'ten'—

he's counting fingers—words a fool can master
in a morning, could be singing in two days,
and maybe 'thank you', or 'see you tomorrow'.
Immigrants, they open shops, Sargon says.

Immigrants open shops, Sargon says,
a teenaged girl perched high on a stool
happy to try the few new words she's learned
after her first week in the local school.

But when they pass through the bead curtains
into the back room, when they step back from the till,
or when friends or family drop by for a taste
of the old country, it's the old language still:

a newspaper lying open on a table,
the TV always on on the high shelf
making the drunk who stumbles in by accident
wonder if he's the immigrant here himself.

Immigrants open shops, Sargon says,
eight years ago already, hard to believe,
the troops back then still gathering on the border
of the homeland he hadn't seen in twenty years.

"One for the road?" he asks. I shrug: "Why not?
As my mother says, we'll be a long time dead."
Sargon smiles: "I'll remember that, my friend,"
but he's far away this evening, lost in himself,

gazing out into our tidy garden
through his pale reflection in the glass,
a nervous shopkeeper as night approaches
hearing ominous voices in the dark.

THE PLAN

On Malahide's light-washed beach
the young couple playing some strange game—
pacing back and forth with sticks and tape,
and not a ball in sight—turn out to be

mapping out the house they plan to build,
its walls and doorways inscribed in the wet sand,
moving from imagined room to room
beneath the setting sun, the rising moon.

WINTER BURIAL

i.m. Liam Brady

Twin jet trails crossing the sky;
here's us frozen in the lake of time
and up there God goes blithely skating by.

'LIGHTHOUSE 1'

after a painting by John Shinnors

Darkness repeats
endlessly. Light
is always new.

THE TUNE

i.m. Pádraig McGrane

Half of the evening
he sat in the kitchen
playing that tune

('Banish Misfortune'
or 'The Spanish Man's Daughter'?
hard to be sure)

barely touching his drink
between cooker and sink
like a monk in a cell

set free by the roll
and the rise and the fall
of some shape-shifting spell

with its endless inventions
and half-baked intentions
till he came up for breath

and some boy in a wig
called for 'The Monaghan Jig'—
and we'd lost him again

A WINTER BLESSING

for Nobuaki Tochigi

Since early evening snow has held us
spellbound at our windows,
erasing our plans, the world itself,
flake by innocuous flake.

'Letters sent from heaven'
the physicist Nakaya called them,
the snow crystals he grew and studied
in Hokkaido before the war,
his camera revealing
miraculous detail
in this deep and wide-thrown
blanket of forgetting.

Across the way, a light goes on
in a room that seems to float
in empty space. Snow
forgets, obliterates, subtracts
(by adding to), yet all the while
asks that we consider
the finer details
of who we are,
of what it is we rely upon
and love—at once

gift and theft, precious
and insubstantial,
and always new,

new as the world the caveman saw
when nothingness flared a moment
on his arm and vanished,

or the king waking up
in his stout-walled castle
impregnable from every direction
but above.

THE INVERSE WAVE

Every sound in the town he recorded:
the river, half full, the kids
in afternoon playgrounds, the fool
stood out on the street to sing,
the believers and all of the certain doomed
driving to work, eating their take-outs,
beached in the mid-summer sun. All of it,
all of them. And late one night he made
a digital negative, an inverse wave
which the following evening he broadcast so loud
on his stereo (driving around
with the windows rolled down and the volume up full)
that its sound cancelled out the originals,
and everything went still:
the factories, the traffic,
the games and the arguments,
the inside and out,
the known world's perfect din and constant roar,
until all that was left was two lovers
in darkness, whispering together
words never uttered before.

READING PAT BORAN

by Dennis O'Driscoll

PAT BORAN DESCRIBES Portlaoise, the County Laois town where he was born in 1963, as "our once congested, now double-bypassed town". Following EU-funded 'bypass' operations, midland towns like Portlaoise are no longer clotted with city-bound traffic. The conference hotel where tight-suited insurance men endure a pep-talk from their regional manager; the shopping centre beyond the church where stubbly farmers, on the way home from a mart, stock up with tea bags and fruit cake; the pallid public hospital: all have reverted to local phenomena. *The Shell Guide to Ireland* judges Portlaoise to be "noteworthy merely as the location of the Republic's only male convict prison"—thus sentencing the town to be bypassed by potential visitors also (except, of course, the involuntary kind).

Portlaoise would have been largely bypassed by literature too, were it not for the fidelity and clarity with which Pat Boran has portrayed the town in his work. County Laois may mean little to the tour guide whose coach passengers are intent on chalking up a sighting of the world-renowned Rock of Cashel rather than the locally-cherished

Rock of Dunamase, or to the executive whose digital organiser burns with the urgency of his next city appointment. But, for those who inhabit the town, it is the centre of the known world. Here they are: the schoolboy who grows drunk on the wine uniform of the girls' school; the widow parking "her black Raleigh / outside Whelan's butchershop"; mourners "escorting / a body down the street"; "the square, / a country town, neighbours / stripped of their professions and their trades, / aprons hung and blinds pulled down, / the accordion band doing its best". And what is a town without its characters? Eddie Boylan of the grocery shop on Lower Main Street is recalling his youth (a "fading world, rich / in an obsolete currency"); the Guru Maguire achieves instant celebrity on a TV chat-show; Hannigan's brother "went to the dance and never / came home again"; a mischievous delivery man is ferrying chickens in a van with "wash-me back doors".

Vividly though the moods and mores of his small town world are captured, there is far more to Pat Boran's poems than what he terms 'footnotes to a local history'. It is not just that, like all good poets, he universalises experience but also that his imagination ranges freely, responding to everything from Dublin street scenes to celestial mysteries. Diverse in theme, wide in scope, modulated in rhythm, his poetry excels at making what Seamus Heaney calls the "transition from the world of data to the words of invention". That Pat Boran would become a poet in the first place seemed almost preordained from the moment in his youth when—proving that the Muse moves in mysterious ways—brochures for the family's travel agency in Portlaoise came packaged with a tour of Miroslav Holub's work:

> One of the first poems to make an impression on me was Miroslav Holub's 'A Boy's Head'. Possibly more than any other, with its great endorsement of the imagination, it marked the beginning of a physical (in the sense that it came from outside my own geographical world) and a mental journey into writing. And the fact that I first came across it on a printer's offcut from some anthology which had been used to wrap brochures for my father's travel agency was poetic in itself.

Perhaps it is to the example of Miroslav Holub, a scientist as well as poet, that Pat Boran owes one of his great strengths—an objectivity which might be described as scientific; an ability to maintain a determined detachment from his subject-matter, to distance his poetical 'I' from an empirical self in order to gain a clearer perspective on the world. Yet his detachment is in no way doctrinaire; tonal warmth and emotional empathy are always on hand where appropriate to a love poem or elegy. Apart from the scientific stance it often adopts towards reality, Pat Boran's work reflects a keen interest in scientific thought itself. Names overheard in his books include those of J.B.S. Haldane, Niels Bohr and Albert Einstein. There are 'Notes Towards a Film on the Life of Galileo Galilei'; an eclipse of the moon is observed through a poetic lens; and 'Bedtime at the Scientist's House' suggests that the raw facts of scientific data cast a story-like spell ("Tell us the names of Jupiter's moons, / the valencies of atoms 1 to 103"). In the poignant 'Waving', childhood recollection unexpectedly segues into scientific epiphany at the precise moment where a cloying note might have been a danger.

When experimenting in his own language lab, Pat Boran—never afraid to risk fragmentary utterances—is more often a poet of implication than of explication. The reader works backwards from the evidence presented as frequently as the writer moves forward towards a final click of narrative closure. From the very start, he triumphed at one of the hardest calls in poetry: gauging when to regard a poem as finished and best left alone. He never overstates or overstays; the poems are remarkable both for their resonance and their restraint. Viewed very broadly, Pat Boran's work falls into two principal categories: poems which chart the human struggle to make sense of our existence on a mysterious planet afloat—maybe even adrift—in space; and those in more direct mode where people are recorded in life, elegised in death or celebrated in love. In the latter mode, he could as justifiably have named his second collection Familial Things as *Familiar Things:* the familiality displayed in poems about parents and siblings breeds unsentimental tenderness, as in 'Song for my Parents':

> Evening sky and age, you do not take them,
> but rearrange the furniture of home
> until they lose themselves among familiar things.

Eight years later, in the tightly-crafted *As the Hand, the Glove,* the familiar things are themselves lost: the old family home is as empty as the shells of the wave-washed 'House of Shells' in his first book ("the tide in its gables almost audible"). The wireless "breaking out into the world beyond / our sleepy, listening midland town / in a house since vanished" is described as "the only thing on earth defined / by absence…Wire-less". The defining absence in *As the Hand, the Glove* is that of the poet's recently-dead father whose 'disappearing act' prompts questions that can never be answered and quests—of recovery and discovery—that can never be fulfilled. Pat Boran writes evocatively about childhood and children. 'Children' is a piercingly perceptive poem, one of his very best; he writes well too of childhood icons like Desert Island Dick, of a "breezy, childhood room made infinite / by conspiracies of movement and light" and of an ostracised, bullied child.

A preoccupation with time, its ravages and ramifications, is what draws together the thematic threads of his poetry—personal and scientific, local and global. The meagreness of the human life-span is all the more evident when set in the continuum of infinity and space. Even language cannot be relied on to preserve what is being lost to ageing and dying: "We feared speech / knowing of the alliance / between language and time". In the opening lines of 'Am', a poem in memory of his father, a watch-face mirrors his own face:

> 1.35 a.m.
> I look at my watch and see
> my life story:
> I thirty-five am …

Somewhat older than thirty-five though Pat Boran now is, his poetry is not at all as well-known or widely-read as it deserves to be. It would be an overstatement to describe him as neglected—his poetry has, from the first, enjoyed the admiration of his peers; he also gained recognition as children's author, festival programmer, editor, reviewer, broadcaster, workshop director—but he is undoubtedly underrated. Hence this attempt to briefly encapsulate his poetical oeuvre as a whole (and not just the selection from it he has made for this book); and, while almost as sceptical about introductions to poetry volumes as I am about cover blurbs, I feel impelled to make a sole exception in this case because of my longstanding conviction that Pat Boran's work merits a large readership and serious critical attention. His absence from many anthologies too is surprising, given how satisfying his poems can be not only collectively but individually (think of 'Song of the Fish People', 'Literature', 'Machines', 'The Dead Man's Clothes', 'The Immortal' and numerous others already cited).

Several years ago, I found myself riveted by a short story set in London and read on the radio (or should I say 'wireless'?) by an actor. I had missed the beginning of the broadcast, and had absolutely no clue as to the author's identity; yet I quickly realized that he or she had writerly skills in abundance. Discovering later that the story was by Pat Boran, I was confirmed in my view that—even on a blind tasting—here was a writer whose talent for language was unmistakable. Perhaps the fact that I had entered the story at its half-way stage was telling in itself: he is a master of writing that plunges its audience *in medias res*. "It's like what happens with water" his third collection, *The Shape of Water,* blurts out with buttonholing bluntness in its first line, not even pausing to remove its sopping hat and hang up its raincoat. Now himself *nel mezzo del cammin,* the timely selection published here allows us to savour a cross-section of Pat Boran's finest work. Author of a chapbook called *History and Promise,* he is also a poet of mystery and fulfilment, of the eternal and numinous no less than the earthly and everyday. Although a spirited celebrator of the local and the known, he steps "beyond / the porch-light of language" to hazard the dark and comfortless unknown.

NOTES

p. 12: 'The Castlecomer Jukebox'. A 'thrupenny bit' is a three-penny coin in pre-decimal currency.

p. 15: 'Master'. "I am no style / and I am all styles"—Bruce Lee's description of his newly invented martial art of Jeet Kune Do which borrowed from many but was also fiercely independent of other martial arts.

p. 55: 'A Creation Myth'. This poem is based on the story of a dinner party, attended by a number of well-known physicists, at which the game of Twenty Questions was played with somewhat unusual results.

p. 57: 'Listening Wind'. This poem concerns a a subject that troubled me as a child: what age will we be if we should ever find ourselves in heaven, the age at which we died or the age at which we were happiest in life? The title, for reasons I don't recall, is from a song by the band Talking Heads.

p. 77: 'Neighbours'. This poem is a roundabout way of recording the migration of many northern Irish families southwards during the worst years of the so-called 'Troubles'. To a great extent, the horrors of what they had experienced on the other side of the border was entirely lost on us ill-informed southerners.

p. 85: 'Literature'. 'Rosebud' is a reference to the movie *Citizen Kane* and, by extension, to the alternative or other possible life that its central character might have lived. Jekyll and Dorian Gray, similarly, refer to other fictional double existences.

p. 86: 'Machines'. The main building of the Royal College of Surgeons in Ireland (on York Street / St. Stephen's Green in central Dublin), though fronted by a well-known classical facade, is for the most part an ugly concrete replacement for the row of Corporation flats demolished to accommodate it. At the time this poem is set, the flats complex on the opposite side of the street still stood (I lived in it at the time), though it too has since been demolished.

ABOUT THE AUTHOR

 Pat Boran is an Irish poet, writer, broadcaster and editor. Born in Portlaoise in 1963, he has long since lived in Dublin. He has published more than a dozen books of poetry and prose, including *New and Selected Poems* (2007), with an Introduction by Dennis O'Driscoll, the humorous prose memoir *The Invisible Prison* (2009), and the popular writers' handbook *The Portable Creative Writing Workshop* (latest edition, 2013). He has edited numerous anthologies, including, with Gerard Smyth, the bestselling *If Ever You Go: A Map of Dublin in Poetry and Song* (2014). He is a former presenter of *The Poetry Programme* and *The Enchanted Way* on RTÉ Radio 1, and awards for his poetry include the Patrick Kavanagh Award and the US-based Lawrence O'Shaughnessy Award. Editions of his work have appeared in Italian, Hungarian and Macedonian. He is a member of Aosdána, the Irish affiliation of creative artists. His most recent publication is *Waveforms: Bull Island Haiku,* a pocket-sized haiku sequence illustrated by the author's own photographs. For further information see *www.patboran.com*.